DANGEROUS INTIMACIES

Poems

by

James Ralston

BLUE LIGHT PRESS ◆ 1ST WORLD PUBLISHING

SAN FRANCISCO ◆ FAIRFIELD ◆ DELHI

Dangerous Intimacies

Copyright ©2025 by James Ralston

All rights reserved. Printed in the United States of America. No part of this book may be used or reproduced in any manner whatsoever without written permission except in the case of brief quotations embodied in critical articles and reviews. For information contact:

1st World Library
PO Box 2211
Fairfield, IA 52556
www.1stworldpublishing.com

Blue Light Press
www.bluelightpress.com
bluelightpress@aol.com

Book & Cover Design
Melanie Gendron
melaniegendron999@gmail.com

Cover Art
Rosalind Brenner

Author Photo
Tim Snyder

First Edition

Library of Congress Cataloging-in-Publication Data

ISBN: 978-1-4218-3597-6

Acknowledgements:

An earlier version of "Out of Our Reach" appeared in *The Sun: A Magazine of Ideas*, in May 2019, Issue 521 Editor, Sy Safransky.

"Begin the Hours of This Day Slow" and "Short Visits Are Usually the Best" were included in an anthology, *All the Men Came and Danced*, 2025, Wyld Syde Press, Editor Tammy Nuzzo-Morgan, Co-editors Diane Frank & Gregory Cioffi.

Some of the prose in "Blindsided" first appeared in *The Choice of Emptiness*, Acheron Press, 1982; and later in *A Bell Ringing in an Empty Sky, The Best of The Sun, Volume One*, edited by Sy Safransky, 1985.

I wish to thank the following individuals and groups:

Blue Light Press and its founder, Diane Frank, for her encouragement to write this book. And for finding it worthy to publish;

Erik Ievins, C.J. Moll, and Barb Hurd, and Holley Ralston for proof-reading;

Rosalind Brenner for the powerful cover painting;

Melanie Gendron for designing the book and covers, which I knew from her past work would be great;

Barbara Schantz Judd, for a month's worth of insightful readings and suggestions, and for the great fun we had in going back and forth;

and huge gratitude to the Finzel ping pong group, Barb Hurd, C.J. Moll, Tim Snyder, and Holley Ralston, for their twice weekly high-level critiques, one poem at a time, two poems a week for more than a year.

There are many others – former colleagues and students, lifelong friends, family members (many also writers and/or artists) – who helped along the way, critiquing a poem, or inspiring me to a new one. Since there is no clear cut-off here, I won't mention names, rather send each of you a copy of *Dangerous Intimacies* with a heartfelt thanks for your strong reading skills and perspectives, for your friendship and time and support, without which this book, "my" book, could not have been written.

In gratitude to and memory of
STEPHEN DUNN
1939 - 2021

If you had a grave, Stephen Dunn,

and I could carve tough love in stone,

I'd sculpt these words of Henry James

under your name, beneath your dates,

as your farewell thought, too,

for us who remain:

Live. Live all you can!

It's a mistake not to.

Contents:

PART I: ON THE ROAD
Getting Used to It 3
Hurt Pigs 5
High School Football 6
Out of Our Reach 7
On the Road 8
Something Human 12
Roughing It 14
Lessons 16

PART II: DANGEROUS INTIMACIES
I'm My Own Worst Student 23
Short Visits Are Usually the Best 24
Levitation Exercises 25
After Acupuncture 26
Relax and Allow 28
Gratitude Hits a Snag or Two 29
Dangerous Intimacies 30

PART III: THE WHOLE MESS, AND THEN SOME
Hanging On 33
Savoir Faire 35
Closet Prayers Overheard 38
Snow in Late April 41
Surprise 43

AN INTERLUDE (for the death of my mother)

"How Great Thou Art" 47
She Found Herself another Hour 52
Us Cairls Can Take It 53
In the Cemetery, and After 55

PART IV: IN MY HOUSE ALONE

How a Movie Can Change a Life 59
Begin the Hours of This Day Slow 61
Did He Who Made the Lamb Made Thee 62
Big, Wannabe Big, and Medium Small 64
Finished 66
A Happy Sisyphus 69
Blindsided 71

PART V: BOW, STUBBORN KNEES

One Less 77
Taking Inventory 78
Upon Hearing the Doctor's Report 81
Modern Times 82
Written in my Sleep 83
One Last To-Do List 84

Afterword: A Eulogy for Stephen Dunn 85

About the Author 95

Part I

On The Road

"For our healing we have on our side one great force: the power of Creation, with good care, with kindly use, to heal itself."
— Wendell Berry, from *The Unsettling of America*

Getting Used to It

Even an abundance of mother love
and father protection can never make
a child's life perfectly safe; only less
aware of the huge troubles coming,

like a clueless frog with a hungry snake
slithering up behind to swallow it alive
on the banks of the river in which later
that summer Benny would drown.

The Michigan winter felt extra cold
in 1957, as we huddled around the stove
thinking of Benny though nobody said it
lest of one of my sisters started to cry.

And if that wasn't already pain enough,
behind the barn was a patch of red snow
where Flora, my pig, was bled to death
by Dad and Uncles Boots and Walt.

They had invited me to watch, I guess,
to toughen me up, to make me a witness
to the man's part in preparing the meat
for the Christmas dinner table.

"Someone has to kill the pig," Walt said.
But this pig had a name, and it was hell
to be there, to watch Flora betrayed,
to hear Flora screaming.

If this was what it took to be a man,
I wanted no part in it, while bit by bit

I grew into one anyway, like it or not.
Come time to slaughter chickens,

while I refused to wield the hatchet,
I did laugh as they ran around headless,
and "let's call that progress," Dad said.
But was it? From an upstairs window

I can see Benny's house over the fields,
looking as though he is still living in it,
the same as mine would look to him,
if he were the one still alive.

Hurt Pigs

In remembrance of Robinson Jeffers' "Hurt Hawks"

Pigs, in the barnyard,
you're smart, Dad says,
but in light of your past,
I've wondered about it,
if you're smart at all.

As feral sows and boars,
you lost your wild ways
in apple orchards, rows
of corn, barnyard mud
to wallow in.

We people now provide
just about your every need,
rotten apples, pails of slop,
table scraps, potato peels,
a pen in a barn in winter.

If you fat boars could talk,
I'd ask, do you still dream
of freer days in the woods,
your fights to the death,
your tusks still intact?

When you're awake, I see
the pain in your small eyes,
and under that, your wrath.
You made a huge mistake
to sell your soul to man,

the best of you now over
before you're even born.

High School Football

Oh, the pleasures of undressing Rebecca
in the backseat of my dad's Plymouth sedan
after a game when I'd made a touchdown,

my fingers now in reach of her treasures,
half surprised she can't stop me either,
or maybe she just doesn't want to.

In the next game, with archrival, Bentley,
I fumbled in enemy territory, was benched,
but quickly forgot it at the Drop In Motel,

in Rebecca's arms for the whole nine yards,
whispering promises that I wouldn't keep,
but wasn't smart enough to keep secret,

as Friday by Friday, now a second stringer,
I consoled myself with the fact that Rebecca
still loved me and she was what mattered,

until later that fall, playing "Truth or Dare,"
I confessed to a promise I'd already broken,
and she shot back with two of her own.

And that was it for Rebecca and me.

Out of Our Reach

At school, in a therapy circle
"recommended" by a counselor,
as my turn to speak comes around
to say what I'm *feeling* right now,
I panic and shoot for the door.

Back home, I offer no explanation
for my early arrival, but go straight
to the toolshed, where I find comfort
in chisels, wrenches, hammers, vises,
tools that I know how to use.

Mom says I'm my dad all over again.
Even the day my friend Benny drowned
I pounded and sawed my way through,
while she lay sobbing in the house.

I recall Dad saying that he felt like
someone had punched him in the gut,
referring to Benny's shocking death,
but also to Mom weeping like that,
out of his reach, and mine, too.

That night, on our walk to the barn
to hand-milk the cows and slaughter
some chickens for the funeral dinner,
I asked Dad why men don't cry.

"You just learn to take it, that's all,"
he said, handing me the hatchet.

On The Road

I

In northern Florida
in a broken-down van
I park near "God's World,"
a commune of nudist vegans
named Light, Sun, Garden,
Butterfly, Flower, Tree,
and so on.

It is the seventies.
No one wants to know
that the sixties are over
and not coming back.

I surely don't want to,
writing every morning,
then hoeing in the garden
on hot Florida afternoons
for a share of the harvest;
and to be honest, to hoe
next to Flower, whom
I've been looking for
most of my life.

II

In a shattered heart
and a bewildered mind
for a long stretch of time
after Flower chose Tree
over me.

In slow, dreary days
in a Seminole chick-ee
with a leaky straw roof
and no running water,
no toilet.

In rooms over bars,
in anger and drugs.

On a long road west,
then south, to a hostel
in Guanajuato, Mexico,
tough city, street tough,
drugs I'm not used to.

Robbed in my room,
punched in the face,
it feels almost good,
the clarity within it
of the victim I play
to my sorrows.

III

Poco dinero, I sleep
for five pesos a night
on the rollaway cot
in the walk-in closet
of a house an amigo
shares with his mom,
"who is totally blind,
and won't even know
that you're in there,"
he promises.

But within a few days
I hear her stick clicking
down the hall, then stop
at my door to give me
a free Spanish lesson:

"Que haces ahí? Quien
se cree usted que es?"

The real questions at last.
What *am* I doing in here?
And who *do* I think I am?
What idea of me is living
as this wretched outsider,
what Kerouac, Ginsburg,
what underground man?

It's a huge wake-up call,
although I'll need a few
more like it, if possible,
kindlier, I thank God
in advance.

IV

Back in Florida, sleeping
in the weedy dunes behind
Crescent Beach, lest Flower
walk by and know who I am,
I'm awakened one morning,
either dying or super alive.

Something was coming.

Then a few yards above me,
nine pelicans in a perfect V
flew over my sleeping bag,
while singing this song
with their wings:

*fit in/ fit in/ fit in/ it's time/
for you/ to find/ a job.*

V

It takes a few weeks
to dump my bad habits,
to afford two false teeth,
to land a job in the sticks
teaching English, *Lucky Jim*,
On the Road and other books
which mean as much to me
as to the students; poetry,
too, Frost my favorite,

although, for a while,
as a matter of survival,
I am determined to take
roads *more* travelled by,
to move with the flow,
to stop looking back,

except, now and then,
at a photo of Flower
hoeing the gardens
of God's World.

Something Human

If we'd but lift up our eyes
into the winter skies, we'd see
Orion, the hunter, rising at dusk
with his club; and bloody Mars,
an immortal god, ready to fight
to the death.

We'd be reminded again
how long violence has been
entrenched in a man's mind
as a big part of his essence.

The Greeks and Romans
glorified war in this same sky
some three thousand years ago.
And coming soon, here on earth,
another war "to end war forever,"
as some men will say to pretend
they love peace.

In times of peace, prepare for war,
is more like it.

So check us off. We are finished,
given the arsenals of nuclear bombs,
the casual talk of sending them on
should the West dare do this
or the East dare do that.

Turn the other cheek?
Forgive your favorite enemies?

That's not how a real man thinks,
unless he's a Jesus, a Gandhi,
a Martin Luther King,

men who never threw a punch
in their lives, as if something else
is more worthwhile than violence,
something higher up on the scale.

Something human.

Roughing It

I'll be damned.
I've fallen in love with a job,
teaching young adults and a few
older ones in rural West Virginia,
poorest state in the union, the only
state where I was given an offer,
having applied nationwide.

Think of it. Being paid to talk
about the work of Anton Chekhov,
Virginia Woolf, Henry Thoreau,
William Shakespeare, no less.

Today, in a survey of American lit,
we're on Whitman's "Song of Myself."
It's huge to love the person you teach,
not only the poetry, but also the poet
who believes that wherever he goes,
with a little mettle, we can go, too,

be it holding the hand
of an enemy soldier who'd otherwise
be dying alone,

or sharing a bed
with a "retarded" brother, and grateful
for his company,

or saying yes
to the breathtaking touch of a friend,
or carrying on, half paralyzed
by a stroke.

"I contain multitudes,"
the good gray poet says.

Don't we all, he implies.

And the more we contain,
the more room we have.

Lessons

Lesson one

In Tennessee Williams'
"The Glass Menagerie,"
the slightly crippled Laura
gets one long kiss from Jim,
a gentleman caller who *knows*
why she's so alone in her life,
the inferiority complex thing.

He'd had one of those himself
before he got some counseling,
found out where his talent was
and took up public speaking.

Private speaking, too, perhaps.
"You're pretty," Jim tells Laura,
"Your eyes are pretty, your hair,
your hands.

"Someone ought to kiss you,
Laura," he says, and then does,
so she will feel pretty; or maybe
so he can forget for the moment
that he's engaged to Betty.

"Some women are pretty upset
if you keep 'em waiting," he says,
soon after the kiss, on his way
to the door.

Lesson two

In Alice Munro's
"How I Met My Husband,"
innocent Edie, sweet sixteen,
experiences older Chris's kisses
on her fingertips, her eyes, her lips
(Edie soon kissing back, and how!),
while they dry-hump on his tent cot,
little chance of stopping them now,
we readers are apt to be thinking.

"Oh, no!" Chris cries, jumping up
to flick water on his face, then hers.
"I wouldn't hurt you for the world,"
he says, and the male half of class
believes that he meant it, the girls
not quite so sure.

The other man in this short story
is a mail carrier with big buckteeth,
who daily looks forward to seeing
Edie's smiling face at the mailbox,
waiting for the promised letter
that Chris never sent.

Carmichael, the mailman, assumes
that Edie's smile is intended for him.
And as she likes people to be happy,
she never tells him otherwise.

So, ever after, as her husband,
he was at peace. But was Edie?
Or did she settle for less?

Lesson three

In Anton Chekhov's "The Kiss"
bespectacled, round-shouldered
and weak-chinned, Ryabovitch,
rarely noticed, and when absent
never missed, makes a quiet exit
at an officer party to find a room
in the basement to be by himself,
to reflect on his zero-sex appeal,
who he cannot be, and who
he has to be instead.

He has barely closed the door,
when in the darkness a woman
seizes him and gasps "At last!",
kisses him as if they are lovers,
then suddenly stops, pulls back,
screams and speedily exits.

Nevertheless, Lt. Ryabovitch,
for several breathless seconds
was a man passionately kissed,
and for a few weeks thereafter
he wants to repeat it, imagines
he can, thinks that it's a matter
of being in the right place
at the right time.

How lost can you get?

Assignment

Compare and contrast these
first kisses, what was learned
and by whom.

Throw in one of your own,
if you wish, a kiss unfollowed up,
what wasn't right, and why not?

Or here's another possible topic.
How does life look down the road
for any two of these characters, *if*
Heraclitus is right and everything
turns into its opposite.

Paint me a word picture of joy
that ends in sadness and regret.

Or turn it the other way around.

Part II

Dangerous Intimacies

"A man who has not passed through the inferno of his passions has never overcome them... Whatever we give up, leave behind, and forget too much, there is always the danger that the things we have neglected will return with added force."

– C. G. Jung, from *Memories Dreams Reflections*

I'm My Own Worst Student

The Greeks accepted that Apollo knew
life's deepest truths. That's why I assign
Oedipus Rex to freshmen every semester,
but also to refresh myself in its premise,
that truth is not so much "figured out"

as seen. And not by a high IQ thinker,
as was the riddle-clever King Oedipus,
but by a person like Teiresias, oblivious
to power and titles, indifferent to riches
and to everyone hiding behind them.

Queen Jocasta laughed at prophecies,
saw Teiresias as old-fashioned, at best,
assumed that she was intelligent enough
to outsmart any scruffy old street priest,
but it's not so easy to skirt around truth.

As she rides her pride to its tragic end,
even the child of this know-it-all queen
will marry his mom if Apollo so sees it,
and then gouge out his eyes the minute
he knows how appalling seeing can be.

Jocasta chooses suicide.

Short Visits Are Usually the Best

I'll be on the road before I know it,
but I still keep my place tidy and clean,
lawn mowed in summer, raked in the fall,
on a remote chance that someone drops by
that I want to see, honks in the driveway,
knocks at the door, and when I open it,

"Oh, Grasshopper," I'd say. "I thought
you would never come. You've lost weight.
You're worn out, I can tell. You're worried.
That makes me worry, too. I'll brew us a tea.
Green tea, if I remember."

And of course I do.

As the water is boiling, I'd dust off my atlas
so she can show me everywhere she has been,
and where she is going next. "My guest room
is free," I'd say, "if you'd like to slow down
and relax a few days.

"After that I can't be sure *I'll* even be here,"
I'd also say, since she knows from experience
how quickly I can confuse her feelings for me
as if they are the same as my feelings for her.

"One sugar or two?" I'm learning to ask.

Levitation Exercises

a few weeks after she moved on

Can this be true?

In my morning solitude,
as I at last break through
to one inch off the ground,
from all confused to peace
of mind, at least moving
in that direction,

I'll be damned if she's
not up there one inch, too,
on an inner hill of her own,
her bluebird all too soon
in restless flight.

And though I've vowed
to not fly after her again,
I'm overwhelmed to hear
her tweeting in the pines,
"Here I am, home free."

"I'm home free, too,"
I caw back like a crow,
as if I'm cracking a joke,
though I'm not, nor is she.

As always, we are both
barely holding our own.

After Accupuncture

He pulls the needles out,
checks my pulse and says
"Your chi is flowing now,"
as if I know what chi is.

On the drive back home,
my latest "friend" Clara
is upset with my mood.
"So what's new?" I ask.
"It's too hot," she says.

But at our stop at the mall
(a quick one she promises),
something *new* is going on.
I feel resilient for no reason
and lighter on my feet, even
as Clara goes clipping along
several steps ahead of me.

"She is she and you are you,"
I hear Ted's voice whispering
as we take our separate paths,
she to a nail salon, I for a fan
I've been wanting to buy us,

but soon swept into the flood
of desperate bargain hunters,
I forget what I'm looking for
while I stand right beside it,
a good looking window fan
for only 16.99, plus taxes.

Ted, who knows acupuncture,
says when his chi starts to flow,
it even finds him parking spots.
Somebody will be pulling out
as he's pulling up.

I rush over to the produce aisles,
as if a higher me is now in charge,
knows what I want and guides me
straight to it, the gluten-free bread,
the avocados for 55 cents apiece,

then to a check-out line with but
one man ahead who lets me cut in,
I have so little, he has so much.

"A saint in disguise," Ted says,
"The sooner we see our brothers
and sisters as Christs, the sooner
we all will be!"

Clara's nails still in progress,
I kill an hour at a Bon Ton sale,
playing customer, trying on pants,
curious to see what chi looks like
in a three-way mirror, no thought
of buying a pair, but at this price
what's to lose!

"Good choice," the clerk says,
ringing me up and reminding me
men's underwear will be half off
on Monday, as if she's been sent
by an on-duty angel to assure me
of the oh-so-numerous blessings
still to come, Clara among them,

or maybe not, Ted winks.

Relax and Allow

It never ends,

the good news for New Agers.
Now to "manifest" what you want,
from a new girlfriend to a new yacht,
you only have to feel worthy of it.

Granted, that part is no small task,
as we've been plugged in from birth
to shame and guilt. But listen up!
Feel is the key word here.

Not to be worthy, but to *feel* worthy.
Not to deserve, but to *feel* deserving,
to love ourselves as we already are,
nothing more wanted or needed.

One up-and-coming New Age pastor
recommends that we look eye to eye
in the mirror and repeat "I love you,
I love you" until it *feels like* we do,

until we relax and allow and forget
that words are used to deceive people,
especially ourselves, far more often
than to speak a hard truth.

Holy Metatron! I try not to doubt
Thee and all Thy New Age prophets
now counting their money for saying
the words we're so desperate to hear,

but something's just not adding up.

Gratitude Hits a Snag or Two

If my body feels good, is flowing along,
my mind is inclined to flow along with it,
happy to be alive within the five senses,
but if it needs a vacation, it takes one.

From when Jo first arrives until she goes,
my thoughts are asleep on a faraway beach,
and I barely know where her skin leaves off
and my skin begins. We like it that way.

We call it love.

But here's the rub; there's always a rub
when the joys of sex are repeated too much.
The sweeter the heaven in those first touches,
the deeper the hell they're bound to stir up

when they're not new anymore, nor is Jo,
who starts showing up late, or in a bad mood
and has to hurry back home to the father
of her children.

A hotter hell still if she stays too long.

Dangerous Intimacies

"Where danger is, there is salvation, also." – Friedrich Holderlin

At night the attic is alive with bats.
Groundhogs that live under the kitchen
erupt into powerful fights now and then.
Sex? Territory? What else could it be?

A copperhead slithers into my bedroom.
How he got in the house I only can guess.
In the maple tree next to the front porch,
a swarm of hornets is building its nest

while I read the paper, and half expect
an angry man to drive by any minute
in his Ford-tough truck, with a rifle
mounted on the cab rear window.

When those hornets started to build
their new home so near to my own,
I thought, okay, give them a start,
then knock it down later,

in that I liked to watch, on occasion
too closely, their new nest expanding.
And if I got myself stung a few times
it was worth it.

As a young man with a curious mind,
I wanted to know the world firsthand,
the pleasures, the pains, the losses,
the gains, the whole mess of it,

and then some.

Part III

The Whole Mess, and Then Some

> *"The sexual act is in time
> what the tiger is in space."*
> – Georges Bataille

> *"Everything that was not suffered to the end and finally concluded,
> recurred, and the same sorrows were undergone."*
> – Hermann Hesse, from *Siddhartha*

Hanging On

Some days I still think of her
and me as an *us*. Walking to town
via Liberty Street, I recall the time
we stopped to kiss in the shadows
of this Methodist Church,

then ended up pressing our fingers
into each other's chest as we argued
about who gave more, who gave less
to our courtship. It would be funny
if not so sad.

It was here under this chestnut tree
that she said I would touch her again
over her dead body, back in the days
we were "having sex" now and then.
"If you have to ask," she would say,
"the answer will always be no."

On this corner of Liberty and Vine,
at the stop sign with bullet holes in it,
I said, "Here's what we have become.
Stopped. No Exit. Children Playing.
No U-Turn. One way. Your way."

That night, all subterfuge and artifice,
we bounced into the Last Chance Saloon,
Karaoke Friday. She sang "I Am Woman,"
I sang "Love Me Tender," for the final line
down on my knees, one arm outstretched
to her face in the crowd, as if I were half

praying for something. "For my darling
I love you, and I always will."

Good acting, I was thinking back then,
given the hearty applause from the women,
and a few friendly laughs from the men.

But now I can see I was just hanging on.

Savoir Faire

In spite of her belittling words,
I still waltz Sophia into her bedroom,
half-pretending to half-understand her
sexual politics. "*La femme* is the boss
in her *maison*," I say to appease her.

Mesmerized by her skinny skin skin,
I'd tell her whatever she wants to hear,
just to touch her "*belle chose*," as they
call it in France where she used to live.

But Sophia's no Miss Forthright either.
Her claim to have seen under the mask
of my "pastoral past," she now insists
was a backdoor compliment.

"Then what's your complaint?" I ask,
"Do I take more than I give?"

"No, but you try too hard not to."

A long pause, as I reflect upon that.

"I try too hard *to please you*?
Is that what you're saying?"

"Yes. It's too weak. It doesn't work.
If your own pleasure doesn't come first,
you end up feeding off mine."

"Feeding off?"

I pull a piece of paper out of my wallet,
a poem she'd written, and not long ago,
titled "My Violin to Your Bass Guitar,"
and read to Sophia her own description
of our crossover moment into the land
of bliss "where nothing else mattered
after that, but that."

"Honeymoon talk. Tonight, it bores me,"
she says as she turns her face to the wall,
and within minutes, I have the "pleasure"
of hearing her breathing drop into a snore
instead of the sounds I'd grown used to
and needed.

When I wake up in the morning, I know
that "it's over," and I now wear the shoes
of the man I had replaced, feeling the loss
from his point of view as well as my own,
as he had promised that one day I would.

I am smart enough to not want to linger
for a crumb of hope in a time such as this,
but when Sophia drops me off at my place
for our last good-bye, I'm surprised to see
the tears welling up in her eyes, too.

"The sex was good; that wasn't nothing,"
she says, in a strange mix of half laughing,
half crying. "It was petty of me to suggest
that it was."

It wasn't everything either, I'm thinking,
scouring my mind to find the right words
to not let this happen, while well aware
that it already has.

As if in a dream, I make a quick exit,
stand on the curb to watch her Peugeot
drive away and disappear into traffic
with Sophia's arm out the window
still waving good-bye.

Emerson says in his most famous poem,
"Give All to Love," *When half-gods go,
the gods appear.*

But not right away. He never says that,
and a full year later, I'm still doing time,
with no gods in sight for as far as I see.

Closet Prayers Overheard

Raised Baptist, a holy roller almost,
Jolie has old-time religion in her bones,
right down to praying in the hall closet,
"for privacy reasons," she claims,
between her and her God.

"Your room is private," I remind her.

"My room is for other things," she says,
and firmly reminds me that my enticement
for her to move in, beyond sharing expenses,
was that this apartment would be her home
as much as mine.

"But what if a friend drops by?" I ask.

"Your Sophia friend?" she asks back,
in response to which I go to my room
and slam the door behind me.

"How's the privacy going?" I snarl
at her in the kitchen a few days later,
having overheard her again "braying
like a mule" in the goddamn closet.

"Praying," she says, stressing the 'p'
"I often forget where I am; even who."

Then for a minute I'm not sure *where*
I am either, although it's more woodsy
than a kitchen; and whoever "who" is,
he's seeing Jolie as if for the first time.

Out of nowhere, she asks me if I like
Saint Joan, by the great Bernard Shaw,
since she'd heard through the grapevine
that I direct plays.

"If you ever do *Joan*, I'd like to try out.
No one could play Joan better than I."

"You would look the part," I respond.
"Does that surprise you?" she says.

Only that question itself, I'm thinking.

A week passes before we speak again.
But in each day of that week, I'm a little
less possessed by my memories of Sophia,
and more aware of Jolie, the way she sways
when she walks; doesn't own a car or phone
or computer; has no friends, as far as I know,
beyond God or Jesus; spends her afternoons
reading good books and praying in closets;
and sleeps in a room so close to my own
I could almost reach out and touch her.

Then out of nowhere, Sophia writes me,
wants to be friends, wants to see me again.
A few hours before, I would have exploded
with joy to receive such a letter, since Jolie
would not as of yet have rapped on my door
as I'm in bed reading "Song of Myself."

She'd knocked to say that when she prays,
she often can't tell when she's just thinking
the words and when she's praying out loud.
And to ask me not to hold that against her
should she, one day, try out for *Joan*.

And I say to Jolie, or perhaps just think it,
*I want to touch you, but it may be more
than I can stand.*

Then we'd be married, Jolie thinks back,
if that helps us resist.

It does, but barely. Hands have minds, too.
But at the last possible second, or maybe
a little bit after, we choose to be friends.

The next morning, she's gone, moved out
and left me a note. "Removing temptation.
Don't try to find me. Am already married
to God."

Snow In Late April

a decade or more later

As we try to settle into middle age,
Mary's up and running every morning
to prepare breakfast, her uncanny way
of showing her love and her distance
in the same move.

My consolation is the Sunday *Times*.
Then outside the window, what a surprise,
snow in late April, big white flakes falling
on yellow forsythia, budding peach trees,
newly mowed grass, as if two seasons
are joining for one last good-bye.

I shout to Mary in the kitchen, "come,
hurry, let's have this moment together."
But by the time she's finished poaching
the eggs, toasting the bread and all that,
the snow has turned back into rain.
There is nothing special to see.

In an angry mood, I want to ask, why,
whenever I'm excited, riding up high,
I'm always up there riding alone!

But there we'd be, in our stand-off again,
where words casting blame always put us.
So I smile and say, "Let's eat them eggs
before they get cold."

What a relief a small smile can bring,
not only to Mary, but also to me.

But not quite.

In my youth I went down swinging hard,
but of late I've been playing not to lose.

Surprise

I'm thinking, should I crank up
my Yamaha only every third day,
so the ride doesn't lose its appeal?

I'm pondering, does that thought
pertain, as well, to Mary and me?
Would we get along better seeing
each other – by intention, I mean –
every other day, or twice a week.
Could this be the missing piece
of the closer life we once had.

When I hopped up on my bike
a couple days after my last ride,
I was rip-roaring to go, without
one negative thought in my head
about her anger at me if I forget
to put the trash out on the curb,

or my even greater anger at her
for how our sex is starting to feel
like reading yesterday's paper.

I recall, before we were an item,
how alive I felt to bump into Mary,
say at Starbucks, have some laughs
together with her and her friends.

or at the state fair, how I shouted
to her from the top the Ferris wheel
to meet me later at the Fun House,

"or maybe the Tunnel of Love,
if you'd prefer," and you laughed
and nodded back a vigorous yes.

I want to feel surprised again
by how happy I am to see you.

Or is that what a Yamaha's for?

An Interlude

for the death of my mother

"... death and love always go together; they never separate. You can't love without death; you can't embrace without death being there."
from *Krishnamurti's Notebook*

"... taken together, life and death constitute a more glorious life than life alone."
– Alan Watts, from *The Meaning of Happiness*

"How Great Thou Art"

In the cancer ward on the top floor of Butterworth Hospital in Grand Rapids, I stand at a window overlooking the late winter landscape, the snow-covered roofs of stores, banks, churches, taverns; the street mix of downsized cars and buses; and on the sidewalks tiny human beings moving as if with great purpose to get where they're going on time.

I'm reminded of a James Thurber cartoon in which several such walkers are taking long, hurried strides, oblivious to the graveyard they're passing in front of.

A few feet from the inside of this window, my mother is dying. Dad sits beside her, sometimes nodding off in his chair while holding her hand. After driving all night, I have to look twice to know she is Mom, now skin and bones, tubes up her nose, her bald head half hidden under a scarf that keeps falling off and Dad keeps putting back on, like some macabre comedy scene.

She doesn't recognize me either, stares at an empty space above my head, calls me by the name of her late brother who died of TB before I was born. "Virgil," she says. "You came, after all." Dad tries to correct her, but she can't be reached.

In low tones, Dad and I catch up a little, how the job's going, that kind of talk. He wants to stretch his legs, and we walk to the parking garage to see what I'm driving these days. "It got you here," he says, then names a hymn Mom wants sung at her funeral, assumes that I know it and I do. "But it's a terrible choice," I say, regretting I said it the instant the words leave my mouth. Dad's eyes narrow. "I wasn't aware you'd been asked," he says. Both of us hurt, we return to Mom's room in silence. I go back to the window to write a poem in my journal.

"How Great Thou Art"
for your funeral hymn, Mom?
Does this "great Invisible One"
ever show up with good news?

And did you not recently say,
both on the phone and in a letter,
that if you had known the depths
of the pain that would be the price
of staying alive a few more years,
no doctor would've touched you!
Does not the same apply to Him?

"How Great Thou Fart!"
I come within a breath of shouting
and giving God a big middle finger,
before a nearby voice makes it clear,
this is Mom's last bow, not mine!

•••

"Just looking out the window," I say to a doctor who has jostled my shoulder to ask if I need anything. I thought I was writing a poem, but he says I've been crying for my mom in my sleep and upsetting some of his clients.

"Clients?"

"You don't have to worry. Your Mom is well cared for," he says, then disappears as if I had dreamed him.

I must have slept for a few hours more, because when I wake up a new shift of cleaning ladies is now in full motion, dusting, sweeping, changing the sheets. One mops the floor not far from Mom's bed, while singing to a Crystal Gayle song playing on a radio across the room. "Some hurts can make you cry, some make you want to die, but some just go too deep for tears."

Either too deep for tears, or poor access to feelings, I'm thinking. My mom is dying, and my eyes are bone dry. From when I was a boy, I was trained in not crying. Dad made it clear that I cried too much, that it was bad for me, and bad for the family, particularly when Mom was sick, which was often why I was crying anyway.

Thank God for Mom's brothers, Walt and Boots, strong men known for winning bar-room brawls, who openly wept now and then. In my whole growing up, they were the only men I ever saw cry. And many times I was the trigger. "My God, Jimmy, you look just like Virgil," Boots would say, and Walt the same thing, or something like it, as they wiped the tears from their eyes. Seeing me, especially by surprise, was both hurtful and joyful to them, as if their beloved brother had stepped out of his grave. The "as if" was what hurt. To feel the joy they had to feel the hurt too. But I knew nothing about that then. I just knew they were men, my uncles, and they cried and I liked it.

And being the spitting image of a family hero, who had died young and died bravely, wasn't shabby either. I loved Dad and his side of the family, Grandpa Roy and Grandma Hazel, their general store, their generosity, how they surreptitiously dipped free ice cream cones to poor boys in Six Lakes, how they learned Spanish so they could talk to the Mexican migrants. I witnessed all that, and much more, but I had a Cairl side, too, and that half of me felt freer, wilder, riskier, got into trouble, cried more than I "should have," a lot of good and bad mixed together.

•••

"How's our little lady doin' today?" I wake up hearing one of the cleaning ladies asking Dad.

"She'll be going home soon," he says.

"Ah, poor darling. She's been a saint to the other patients here.

To all of us. What a great wife, you have, sir. We have all come to love her. May God give her rest."

Overhearing Mom lavishly praised stirs up my emotions. Well, thank God, is my first thought. I guess I've still got some. But think again, I tell myself. I sense a flood coming.

"I think I have to go," I tell Dad.

"Go ahead. Take a break. I can see that you need one."

"I mean I have to go home."

"What? Home? You just got here. Come on. I didn't mean to hurt your feelings."

"No, no. I was in the wrong. Mom's choice of hymns was none of my business. It's just that … final exams start tomorrow," I try to lie, but I see right away it's not going to work.

"Are you all right? What's wrong?"

"I just have to go."

"Well, don't get yourself fired, I guess," he says, offering his hand. "I'm sorry we fought."

"It's nobody's fault. These are tough days."

"Don't you want a few minutes alone with Mom. You'll never see her again, you must know that."

(I'm not seeing her now, I'm thinking. She's not seeing me either. Nobody's seeing anybody.)

"Let her sleep," I say, in a raspy voice sounding like someone I might know, but not me.

"Then go, but don't leave without saying good-bye. Mom will be hurt. She won't understand. Don't let that be her last memory of you."

"You tell her for me, Dad. I need to go now, while I'm still able."

On the marble hall floor, I hear my shoes clicking underneath me, as if someone else is walking in them, someone who wants to turn around and go back, but to where and for what he cannot say.

In the elevator, going down, I can't feel my body under my clothes. An off-duty nurse rides down with me, practicing her smile in a compact mirror as she puts on a pink shade of lipstick.

Her lips are moist, almost wet, almost red.

She Found Herself Another Hour

Three days later, much further north,
in the Marion United Methodist Church,
now overflowing with family and friends
standing to sing "How Great Thou Art"
over Mom's dead body.

Sure, I sing along with everyone else,
but give the hymn my private meaning
that it's not God who's great, but Mom,
and her dear friends of oh too solid flesh
who raise the roof right off the church,
their love for her enlarged in grief.

And as the last "Thou Art" is sung,
and sobs are flowing like a contagion
from Opal to Audrey to Pearl to Wava,
and even the men are wiping their eyes,
that new *private meaning* begins to ask
a new question: when people are great,
is God great too?

How smart thou wert if that be true.

Us Cairls Can Take It

The Service is over,
the praise, the eulogies,
the hymns, Bible readings
on life everlasting,

death but a soul passing
from earth onto heaven,
nothing to it, if you're
a believer.

Unseen, I stand alone
at the back of the church,
in the thin afternoon light
of a stained-glass window
of the perfect baby Jesus
in mother Mary's arms.

In the next window over,
Jesus the man raises the dead,
while up front, the undertaker,
Mr. Fosnaught, lowers the lid
on your satin lined coffin until
the last ray of light disappears
on your face, and then "click,"
you're locked into darkness
forever.

And though I didn't expect it,
it was a click I needed to hear.
Outsiders need closures, too,
something true we can feel.

What else clicked inside me
was Uncle Virgil's last gasp
to say goodbye to his family
gathered around his bedside
as he died of TB in 1940.

"Us Cairls can take it,"
were the last words he spoke
to his brothers, Walt and Boots,
but his last words to my mom
he spoke through his eyes.

I was already eleven
when she first told me
of this eyes-only good-bye
in the hour of his death.

"What did his eyes say?"
I asked Mom back then,
but she couldn't answer,
only looked at me oddly
and started to cry.

"It's the only time Virgil
and I ever wept together,"
she told me, as she and I
cried together, our only
time ever, as well.

"To walk away, to let him
die by himself with no one
to hold him, it wasn't right,
but I did it," she said.

"He had asked me to."

In the Cemetary, and After

In March, in Michigan,
the February snow still lingers
on the dark sides of tombstones,
while robins sing and daffodils
bloom, a wintry spring mix.

"She lives in God's house now,"
my beloved sisters, Joan and Jean,
whisper to me near Mom's grave.

Across the way, I see my father
and brother, Jon, and other men,
my uncles, cousins and brothers-
in-law "taking it," being strong
men at their best.

I join them, shake their hands
slowly, firmly. Eyes on eyes,
I claim a place for a moment
in the house where men live
and few words are spoken.

Then no longer knowing
who I am or where I'm going
(if it happens, or if I dream it),
I walk to town, hoping to find
my long-ago Rebecca, who was
speaking to me through her eyes
at Mom's funeral, asking me if
I had enough left-over feelings
to make love one more time.

It wasn't right, but we did it
on the back seat of her Chevy
in the Ideal Bar parking lot.

Pain became one with pleasure,
and after all was said and done,
we cried like newborn babies
in our new mother's arms,

then went our own way
to live our own lives.

Part IV

In My House Alone

*Word I was in the house alone
Somehow must have gotten abroad,
Word I was in my life alone,
Word I had no one left but God.*

from "Bereft" by Robert Frost

How a Movie Can Change a Life
    after Pawel Pawlikowski's *Ida*

Two thousand years ago,
the Romans would have prized
the same sky I'm watching tonight,
a waning Luna aligned with Jupiter
and, once again, almost touching.

It's a near repeat of a sky I saw
ten years ago from this lawn chair,
smoking this same cherry tobacco,
the scent that Laura most loved.

I live alone now, but back then
I shouted up to her, my betrothed,
my Juliet, leaning over the balcony
into what I was soon to find out
was her own private dream,

"Look up at the sky, Laura!
Luna and Jupiter are about to kiss."

"And after that?" Laura asked.

At first I was tempted to laugh,
thinking she was making a joke,
echoing Anna's "and after that?"
to Lis, to his marriage proposal
in *Ida*, a movie we'd watched
downtown the night before.

Lis was a handsome jazz musician,
a talented man at peace with his life.
Though Anna's question alerted him

to a problem, he had a ready answer.
They'd travel, see the world.

"And after that?" Anna repeated.

"Buy a house, have children, pets.
Life as usual," he said.

"And after that?" she kept asking,
long after Lis should have known
he'd already lost her, that the life
he wanted to offer wasn't right
for Anna, who'd lost her parents,
a brother, and everything else
in the Holocaust, except for,
maybe, her God.

I, as well, ran out of answers
to Laura's doubts and questions,
but even as she was packing to go,
I was trying to change her mind.

"Let's take a break from each other,
and see how we feel down the road."

Or, speaking more philosophically,
"What about the 'eternal recurrences'
that we see when we watch the sky?"

"They'd take too long," Laura said,
on her way out the door.

A man knows when he's licked,
but even now, several years later,
Luna and Laura, just before dawn,
can still cast one hell of a light.

Begin the Hours of this Day Slow

    after Robert Frost's *"October"*

October's over, but the deciduous trees
are still in full color, the afternoons warm,
nights brisk for good sleeping, my mind
still embedded in summertime dreams.

And although I'm a little more ready
than I was last year to embrace the end
of this life as the only possible pathway
to a new beginning, I still get cold feet
and can't bear to face it.

I see the Grim Reaper as unqualified
to sweep me aside, as not to be trusted
to know my true value, anything lasting
about me at all. So no, I'm not ready
to be set aside quite yet, thank you!

"Everyone wants just one more year,"
I fondly remember my father joking,
at age 82, the year that he died.

"Then one day you wake up ninety,
or even a hundred; nobody knows you,
nobody cares to. So why linger on
when it's your time to go?"

If not this fall, then certainly next.

Did He Who Made the Lamb Make Thee

Of course He did.
That's the way creation works.
Eat, then be eaten. Why would we
think we're above it?

And Tyger likes his lamb lean,
as do most human beings. Meat
close to the bone where it's tender
and sweet.

A fasting Buddha, not a fat one,
would be Tyger's second best meal.
And third, perhaps, a skinny poet,
a Keats, a Lawrence, a Thoreau.

Two thumbs up. Bon appetite!
Even made-up guys, like Tolstoy's
woeful Ivan Ilyich, would be fine
dining for leeches and parasites,

ferocious eaters, just like tygers,
like black holes, like us, like God.
If we're truly made in His image,
He too has to eat to survive.

What a demented foolishness
our esteemed lives must contain,
as we run barefoot on the beaches,
or, in old age, play singles tennis,

or lift dead weights, ad nauseam.
What in God's name are we doing
but preparing a banquet for worms,
for our second coming of nothing.

Since we humans write the script
and make up everything anyway,
can't we do better than this?

Can't we do better than God?

Big, Wannabe Big, and Medium Small

I

Who is to judge, but it's so obvious:
some folks are given big tasks to achieve,
a Gandhi, Malcolm X, Martin Luther King,
Crazy Horse, Joan of Arc, Ethel Rosenberg,
martyrs burned alive or shot or electrocuted.
Who remembers even a few of their names?

Jesus was killed by slow torture for saying
he was God, although his standing between
an adulteress and those ready to stone her
was most certainly also a factor.

II

Then wannabe big, like you, my friend,
with your many causes, your care for others
for which you are praised to the heavens.
But were you ever in trouble with the law,
say, marching for human rights in Birmingham,
or standing up and being counted for anything
at a cost to your comfort?

III

Then medium small, a person like me,
who attends to little things, the cat, the car,
who brings home the bacon, mows the grass,
is a good neighbor and helpful when needed,
builds his grandchildren a new swing-set –
maybe cheats on his taxes a little bit,
but who doesn't?

"It's a hard life. So many ways to lose it,"
God's clerk will say, making conversation
as she examines her notes, and grimaces.

"And the verdict?" I ask.

"It's like in the Bible, that rich young ruler
who hoped that to tithe would be sufficient.
Please join the crowd in the field to our left.
The big one. You really can't miss it."

"I'm guilty, you're saying.
No mulligans? No second chances?"

"Second chances apply only to Hindus.
Now if you'll step aside, the long line
never ends, and I'm exhausted.

"First tell me where that crowd is going."

"Where do you think they are right now?
Who do you think I am?"

Finished

> *"Body and Shadow comfort one another,* says classical Chinese wisdom." – Anne Carson

If you're an old man, rarely noticed,
say your name is Danny, though nobody
knows it, and you're sitting alone at Lindy's
on Tuesday, spaghetti and meatball night,

you still have yourself to talk to.

This may entail a few awkward moments
while you warm up with some easy stuff,
like weather and sports, always so needed
before a person jumps into deeper waters,

like what's going on in Palestine and Israel,
the Ukraine and Russia, human slaughters
we support with our taxes, merciless wars
toward which we've grown numb.

"Oh, Danny boy, let's not talk politics,"
a less stressed *other you* might respond,
especially if he's just arrived from a bar,
or a Reiki massage or a group meditation.

"Then *you* choose the subject, why not!"
Danny boy snaps back. "What will it be?
The loss of another friend who has died?"

"Let me share a thought with you, Danny.
Grief is a choice. It's something you need,
an isolation that makes you feel superior,"
the other Danny (call him *Donny*) says,
vying for Top Dog, as he loves to do.

Danny: *(under his breath)* "Screw that kind of language! If you've just 'shared' something with me, where the hell is it?"

Donny: "It's an idea. It's in your head."

Danny: "Sorry. It wasn't worth keeping."

Donny: "Too bad for you then."

Danny: "I can't imagine why! Listen. I want your company, not your advice. We know each other, read similar books, back similar causes. We're soul brothers who know how to talk, would never say the word "share," unless it meant giving away part of something we could've had all to ourselves. And we're not so simple-minded, I trust, as to suggest that to feel isolated is what a person might want!"

"Calm down, calm down, take a breath."

"Au contraire, we're two human beings who, on any day of the week, can unpack the complex, make it sound like a poem, and, if I may say so, in perfect English!"

At which precise moment, Henrietta, the waitress, approaches their table to ask, "Are you'se done here yet?"

Donny smiles and winks at Danny. Neither of them would talk that way. Danny subtly corrects her by saying,

"Are we finished? What think you,
Donny Boy?"

Donny replies (since he's already had
one too many, and likes to be funny),
"Not yet, Etta. But if you'se closing,
what say we go out on the town!"

Happily, Henrietta joins in the banter,
and Danny slowly begins to feel better,
having uncovered the *Donny* within him
who knows how to play, how to be light
now and then, a regular guy at Lindy's,
on spaghetti and meatball night.

A Happy Sisyphus

He had his fifteen minutes of fame.
When the old man within showed up,
and he was no longer a plausible hero,
he resigned himself to playing villains,
was cast for one as an unchaste priest,
a seducer of nuns and rich widows.

It was a surprisingly easy transition.
His next step down was the bungler,
the bank robber who shot off his toe,
then a rustler with existential angst
that genuine horse thieves booed
and sexy cowgirls laughed at.

B films paid the bills for a while,
along with the occasional Triple X.
His last girlfriend, whom he first met
as Aphrodite across his Hephaestus,
moved up to become the director,
then reduced his parts to bits.

Broken, he returned to the stage.
His first big role was Walter Mitty,
but the audience booed and groaned
as he flicked away his last cigarette,
and barked out to the firing squad:
"Let's get this dying done!"

And that was pretty much it.

In the death throes of dementia,
he gets to play Sisyphus every day.

A reviewer who knows Greek myth
says that "he's far more convincing
pushing the rock up the hill again
than watching it roll back down.

"What kind of simpleton would smile
in that moment?" he asks in his column
in the *New York Times*. "Since Sisyphus
must know his punishment never ends,
what in God's name would he have
to be happy about?"

Blindsided

I

What would it take to live in steady contact with our deepest uncertainties?" Dane would ask questions like that on our long winter walks. *"Is it even possible to live in our depths, amid the myriads of distractions and escapes with which shallow life baits us? When chaos shows up to play its part in our lives, can we stand up to it and not run away?"*

That he was starting to lose at chess
was an early sign of Dane's decline.
He'd pick up an officer off the board
to ask, again, what a piece was called,
then put it back on the wrong square.

It especially upset him to forget names,
be it a rook, a composer like Mozart,
a world-changing thinker like Marx.

"For Christ's sake, I taught the man!"
he'd exclaim, after I'd reminded him
of Marx's name for the fiftieth time.

Common nouns were the next to go,
then verbs. I could discern in his eyes
his hunger to discuss this brutal night
into which he'd been thrust, a dancer
without legs, a painter without hands,
"a thinker without words" is how he
expressed it, before "it" got worse.

Although language had always been
Dane's greatest gift – not anymore!

He'd forget "Alzheimer's," the word
itself, sometimes my name as well
(and sometimes me altogether).

He'd go upstairs to fetch a book,
and forget what he was looking for,
and that I had stopped by for a visit.
I'd have to shout up the stairwell
to remind him that I was there.

"We should just laugh at it?"
he would recommend to me later,
but I couldn't even crack a smile.

II

Dane was like an older brother to me. He would urge me outwards, challenge my eyes to focus on the world out there, if for no other reason than to give myself another picture, another view of the world inside of me. We developed metaphors for our journeys. We were like Stanley searching for Livingstone, who was searching for the source of the Nile. Or we were like Cortez landing in Mexico and burning his ships, the bridge back to the old world and old things. And nothing was beyond our laughing about, including the absurdity of everyday life, and then death.

On his brutal trip downward,
I visited Dane at every stop along
the way to the bottom, "Total Care"
in Lonaconing, Maryland, where
I read to him from his books.

Soon after he died, Dane began
to visit me in dreams, memories,
mostly pleasant places, but one
which felt more like a curse.

His invitation "to laugh at it"
was painful to remember, because
we could have God-damn done it,
right then, when he said it, laughed
together over his absurd decline.

Laughter had been the ground floor
of our friendship for over fifty years,
not snorting and grinning, but down
on the carpet, holding our stomachs.
And what could have been funnier,
more laughable than Alzheimer's
for a man as smart as Dane was.

Right there and then was our chance
to become the two laughing buddhas!
But I had this mask stuck up my ass
that he was the one with dementia
and I was the one who wasn't.

III

To live on the ocean floor of our being was our theme that first winter of our friendship. We would be Jonahs and get to know ourselves within this strange new world, among these weird unknown shapes and deep-sea creatures. In the belly of the whale, as friends, we would face down the darkness, the difficulties too great to face alone, and from which the human world, on its surfaces, runs away without knowing it.

I've missed several boats in my life,
and one that I didn't, which sank.

Part V

Bow, Stubborn Knees

"There is a tendency at every important but difficult crossroad to pretend that it's not really there. We like to imagine we've already crossed a bridge or not yet come to it."
– Bill McKibben, from *The End of Nature*

"All may be well," says Claudius, in *Hamlet*

One Less

"Men must endure their going hence, even as their coming hither,"
says Edgar, in *King Lear*

"Ripeness is all," Edgar also says.
Did he forget that ripe precedes rot.

The wisest man that I'll ever know
died in a village nursing home bed,
not knowing my name or his own.

Near the end, when I visited him,
he'd grasp my hand for a crumb
of comfort, his breaths counting
down, one less, one less,

death taking its time,
like a cat with a mouse.

"As flies to wanton boys
we are to the gods; they kill us
for their sport," one less, two less,
three less, four, as we breathe on
in fear and trembling, whether
we're the one who is dying
this time or just playing
the role of a witness.

Taking Inventory

My grandson, a second grader,
is the poet who doesn't know it,
walking around the family home
saying "Mama's a girl, I'm a boy,
Daddy's a boy, Auntie's a girl,"
sorting out the shadowy divide
half hidden under his clothes.

If that wasn't challenge enough,
Link, his cat, was totally flattened
in front of his eyes by a red truck
a few days ago; so lump death in
with his gender questions.

"What does it mean to be dead?
If Link can die, can I die, too!"

Inspired by Andrew's perspicuity,
later that day, in my bedroom alone,
before I slide into my afternoon nap,
I take a lengthy look at the old man
in the mirror, one piece at a time.

I am my hands; they aren't bones
idling in a grave. They still can turn
the pages of a book, or even garden
when it doesn't rain or get too hot.

I am my ears, and, although I do
wear a hearing aid, they can hear
"Moonlight Sonata" more clearly
than when they were young.

But who is this *I* that is listening?
That's a question I've been asking
since I was Andrew's age, and at 81
I don't know a whit better than he
what it means to be dead, beyond
I don't want to be. Or not yet.

I am my feet, my legs. I can't run
but I can still walk to the mailbox,
and, so far, without using a cane.

And if my eyes can't see perfectly,
they're aware that the new *mailman*
is a good-looking woman, probably
mid-to-late sixties.

(Like Andrew, but decades ago,
I did some of my homework, too.)

And, even better, when her eyes
chance onto mine, then brighten
into a smile sweeter than friendly,
nine times out of nine I respond
in kind, but I'm not at all sure
what's going on here.

Whatever surprise I may be in for,
now back home in my room again,
I tip my new hat to a happier face
looking back at me in the mirror.

If I'm in over my head, my head
seems not to care. My last dance?
Could she make it happen
this late in the day?

Or has it happened already,
and I'm only starting to know?

Upon Hearing the Doctor's Report

I've been this way since college,
a hard agnostic who quietly smiles
at the belief in God as anything but
a wishful thought, a denial of death,
a band-aid, a fantasy.

But when the bad news is personal,
as it's bound to be for every one of us
now and then, I drop down on my knees
and pray as though I'm a child of a God
I address as my Father in Heaven.

And since this Father to Whom I pray
values honesty most, as my own dad did
when I was his kid, I try to make it clear,
up front, I am not a True Believer yet,
but I have no place else to go.

Ninety-nine out of a hundred proud men,
if in enough pain, will follow the crowd
and pray in God's name, while secretly
wishing they were brave enough not to,
and hoping like hell that nobody sees.

Modern Times

"Where else can we go?" Peter
queried Jesus, who'd asked his men
(before the world knew them as saints,
and He was not quite yet the full Christ),
to keep the faith in the face of death
by torture that awaited them.

But that was a hell of a long time ago,
before the world believed in progress,
cars, trucks, airplanes, drones, rockets,
nuclear bombs to keep enemies at bay;

before TVs, computers, space travel,
longer lifespans, then heated coffins,
an ever-increasing standard of living
in countries already richer than sin;

before every tidbit of information
became almost too easy to access,
and thus too easy to also forget.

Let's ask A.I. Who was Peter?
What was his question again?

Ah, yes. Now I remember.
Where else can we go?

Written in My Sleep

Even in pain, to concentrate
on the target, on God's big heart,
is what it takes. How can I miss
a bullseye this large,

if I will only still my mind,
draw the bowstring slowly, slow,
keep the eyes wide open, wide,
relax the fingers on the cord,
and then let go,

just let that arrow fly.

One Last To-Do List

Read, reread the masters,
who have put their souls
into words, into books,
and left them behind,

Thoreau and Whitman,
to name two of mine.
There are many more,
too many to mention.

But as times worsen,
read Bill McKibben's
The End of Nature.
And *Silent Spring,*
by Rachel Carson.

Bow, stubborn knees.
Pray for forgiveness.

Afterword: a Eulogy for Stephen Dunn

Spoken at City Place, Frostburg, Maryland, in October of 2021

Twenty-some years ago, in 2002, when Stephen arrived in Western Maryland to live here, he was on top of the world, writing the first love poem in his life that had no qualifications; no ifs, no buts, as he told me later. That poem was in reference to Barbara, of course. He moved here to marry and live with Barbara, and, direct quote, "had there been nothing more, that would have been enough."

But, to continue that quote one more sentence: "At that time I had no idea how rich the local community would also become to me."

Not a bad reflection on us, I'd say, from such a big hitter in the world of writing. For as we all well knew, before our first handshake with Stephen, there was a second reason he was on top of the world in 2002. He'd recently won the Pulitzer Prize for Poetry. The gold medal. Or to run further with the big-hitter metaphor, in the world of poetry he had received recognition on the order of the Most Valuable Player in the American League.

And if poetry was the literary form most of us knew the least about, we knew what the Pulitzer Prize was, and we knew that someone on the order of a Mickey Mantle (Stephen's childhood hero, by the way) or more modernly, a Cal Ripken or Ken Griffey was living in a nice but modest home in eastern Garrett County, putting his pants on one leg at a time, getting his haircut at Dugan's Barber Shop, playing poker in a multi-table game in Clarysville, or tennis with the top guns at Rawlings Tennis Club, or ping pong right here at City Place or on Tim Snyder's basement table.

Sometimes we were proud, too proud perhaps, to be suddenly rubbing elbows with a famous person, as when the clerk at a local liquor store introduced him to another customer as the winner of the Nobel Peace Prize. (Stephen got a big kick out of that one, too.) And lord forgive her the faux pas. Who among us wasn't knocked off-kilter, at least a little bit, in the presence of … well, in the world of letters, in the presence of royalty?

Whether we made proudly too much of it, or proudly too little, our first encounters with Stephen were with a reputation as much as with a person. There was no way around it, and one of my early tasks was to read, with critical eyes, some Stephen Dunn poems. Maybe he'd just lucked out or knew the right people. Not every high-level reputation is earned, I reminded myself. But no. He was good. More than good, he was great. His poems jumped off the pages as if they were alive.

Frostburg's writers' group, founded by Barb, Karen Zealand, and the late Doug DeMars back in the mid-1980s, and meeting bi-weekly in Barb's (and now Stephen's) living room became my regular time and place to "deal with it." The old order had been overnight shot to hell, but it didn't take long for the upside of working with Stephen to appear. For openers, he was a generous listener, and he wore his reputation neither too proudly nor too humbly. He liked our group and seemed confident that in time we would like him.

And add to that, the bar for writers in Frostburg, Maryland had been raised. To jump over it, we had to get better. Fortunately, like osmosis almost, to be in the same room with Stephen was a step in that direction. The close attention that he paid to sound comes to mind. Of course, we already knew that a poem is a kind of music, has rhythm, in modern poetry half rhyme so subtle that the reader might not know it's there. Good sound traces, Stephen would call them. But he would go so far as to say that if the sound is off in a poem, the meaning will be off, too. It seemed foolish to me, at first, that there could be a connection that intimate between a poem's sound and its meaning, although now, nineteen years later, it's one of the first things I try to get across to creative writing students.

In short, it took some time to absorb Stephen's approach to poetry. It was a full U-turn from the Romantic view I had long espoused – you know, Wordsworth, "Poetry is the spontaneous overflow of powerful feelings, recollected in tranquility." Nothing doing, for Stephen. "In a quality poem, your powerful feelings don't count," he would say. "Understate them. Or better yet, leave them out, let the reader infer them. And as for radical, or noble sentiments, they're worthless without strong counterpoints. And should there be a dialog, an argument, in your poem between a voice who thinks like you do and a voice who thinks more like your nemesis, give your nemesis the better lines."

So much of how Stephen thought about writing was counterintuitive. "Finding a starting place is a blessing," he'd say, "but you don't have to stay true to it. If you get stuck, say the opposite. Feel around. Find out what the poem wants to say. Finally, it's not even your poem." For Stephen, a certain neutrality within the poet for the poem to flow through was the best of all possible worlds.

It was a neutrality embedded within the very physicality of his writing process, which he was circumspect to talk about, but over time I learned some things. In his office, he would remove himself as far as was possible from all distractions, even closing the curtains so that his whole world was the poem he was writing. If it was a new poem, he'd often start it with a prompt, an off-the-top-of-the-head line that a fellow poet had given him to get the poem moving. The real inspiration did not precede the poem but came in the process of writing it. For Stephen the greatest moment in that process came when the poem first surprised him with a line, an image, a metaphor that he hadn't anticipated, that just happened, that more or less had written itself.

The first time that a poem surprised him was big for Stephen. Now he knew he had a keeper on the line. If a poem never surprised him, he knew it was no good. The surprise is a moment in writing, he said, "where we find ourselves saying what we didn't know we knew or couldn't have said in other circumstances."

But in terms of the whole poem, that first surprise, even the whole first draft, was barely to get his big toe wet. Next would come the revisions. Refinements. Reversals. More surprises. More refinements. The more spontaneous a poem feels to the reader, Stephen would say, the longer, most likely, it has been labored. You have to work hard at being spontaneous.

Stephen loved such ironies. To him, life's opposites were inextricably woven together. The yin with the yang, the trough with the wave, the bottom with the top. When he came here to live, as I said, on top of the world, he had also been living with Parkinson's for a long time already. In 2002, the likelihood was five more years, his doctor told him. In a poem that he writes about it, "five years" was what he said he could promise Barbara, in their early discussions of marriage.

But irony, irony. Does Stephen – *does anybody* – ever rise to his or her creative heights, without the Parkinson's or something akin to it? Stephen never said this, but I can easily imagine him thinking, okay, if I only have a short number of years left, I'm damn well going to live them. I'm here now, am I not? If I'm going to worry, I'll worry about the poem I'm trying to finish, not about how much time I have left to live.

And isn't it also possible that at least part of the reason Stephen and Barbara not only got those promised five years, but then another five, and then another, and then one year short of still another. Well, irony, irony, what greater promise for a tomorrow can there be than a today fully lived in "the despoiled and radiant now." That's how Stephen worded that promise in the second of his two "Postmortem Guides," subtitled *"Once again for my eulogist in advance,"* in which he says that "even if we've known despair, it's possible/ with some luck and some love to wander, / sometimes happily, in the despoiled and radiant now." He then quickly concludes his advice to his eulogist with these three lines: "End that way, because the whole truth/ as I've tried to say before/ is nothing anyone has to know."

Well, right you are, Stephen, but with your poems, as with your life, there's always been so much to interpret. Not only is the whole truth nothing anyone has to know, but it also doesn't exist. I'm pretty sure that's one of the ways you meant that line. Or if it does exist, we'll never get our minds around it. The whole truth, if it comes at all, comes to us in surprise little pieces, and from different directions, from over here a little piece, from over there a little piece, and often when we least expect it.

Stephen told me one day, almost off-handedly, that you can't be a writer unless you're also *not* a writer, by which I took him to mean that a writer can't live life to write about life. Because that wouldn't be living life hard enough. To be a good writer, you have to have found your own ways of living hard, and to be living hard all over the place.

That was a little piece of truth that Stephen passed on to me, not only in the words that spoke it, but in how he embodied those words. Life excited him. He loved. He hated. Not to bring politics too much into it, but nobody could hate a recent ex-president better than Stephen could. He thought hard. He argued hard. He swam hard in the depths of life. And, not to forget the shallows, he played ping pong hard. He played poker hard. He even watched television hard.

I will never forget watching with him a documentary built around the Mohammed Ali/George Foreman fight in Africa, where Ali, against all odds, regained the heavyweight title he had been stripped of seven years before, for refusing to be drafted into the Vietnam debacle. Stephen cried the whole way through it, and I know why. Ali, now past his prime, had transcended himself. "Especially in sports, and writing," Stephen once said in an NPR interview, "there was the possibility of transcending yourself, of doing what you couldn't do." Whenever he saw this self-transcendence happen in others, or experienced it within himself, it moved him in the core of his being. In that way, especially, Stephen was an everyday and local model of a man leaving nothing on the playing field, of leaving nothing that was worthy of living, and that he was capable of living, unlived.

In the end I learned more from Stephen about living than about writing; and much of it in his last few years, and especially in the days of his physical decline. By then Stephen, C.J., Tim and I had been playing twice-weekly ping pong games in Barb's and his garage for maybe fifteen years. Stephen started out as the best. He was a natural athlete, and, as with every other part of his life, he gave every game his all. At the Yaddo Artists' Retreat, which he frequently attended for three weeks in the summer, he'd gone undefeated for twenty years in the post-dinner ping pong games. In our garage game, he'd find your weakness and relentlessly exploit it until it wasn't a weakness anymore. And then he would find another one, and you'd have to master it. On and on. To play in that mix, you always had to get better.

In one of his poems, he says that there's no greater insult you can give a man than to lower your level when you play against him. But, alas, human beings are given only so long to live at the apex of their lives, *especially* should that apex be at the top of the world. In due time, Stephen's "despoiled and radiant now" included one of us wheeling him out to the garage in his wheelchair, sometimes through rain, sleet, and snow. And when it was his turn to play, one of us would wheel him into position, help him up onto his feet, and with his left hand resting lightly on the table for balance, he would give it his all, and we all knew better than to let up on him.

He would have brought to the garage with him a poem he was working on for his new book, his last book, *The Not Yet Fallen World*, and handed it to one of us not currently playing to read. If his body was in decline, his creative mind was stronger than ever, in my opinion; if a dying star in table tennis, Stephen was a supernova in his writing.

Those twice-weekly ping pong nights also included an after-game combination of conversation and joking around in the house. We'd have dinner delivered from Eastern Express, or Barbara would cook, or C.J. or Tim would bring something. Often what we were talking about reminded Stephen of a poem, and he'd pull, say, a Robert Frost book off the shelf and have one of us read it.

And when I was one of the listening, I'd might be half-wondering if Robert Frost's friends and neighbors, when they were invited into his home a century ago, were aware that they were in the presence of a man whose poems would be read and appreciated a hundred years hence.

And if it was one of Stephen's poems being read aloud, I sensed that we'd all step back inside ourselves and let it sink in more deeply, the despoiled radiant now of such a moment. For we knew, but at the same time didn't know, how near to the end Stephen's clock was ticking. On the ping pong table earlier, reaching for a shot, maybe he'd taken a fall onto the hard cement floor. Such falls were becoming more frequent, to the degree that Tim had jerry-rigged a harness out of a back-brace tied to a rope strung through a big hook screwed into a beam above the table. Then one of us not presently playing would sit off to the side and hold that rope taut.

But Stephen wearing a harness? That experiment didn't last long.

When Barbara showed up at the garage one May afternoon to tell us that Stephen wouldn't be playing today, we were prepared to hear that. What we weren't prepared to hear was that he'd chosen not to treat the urinary tract infection he now had, nor to take further medical treatments of any kind; in short, that he had decided to die.

"We're in uncharted waters, here," Barb said. "Stephen and I have talked it over many times of late. He feels he's lived a rich life, accomplished within it what was in him to accomplish, enjoyed what was in him to enjoy. He feels it's time for him to go."

Needless to say, that was a different kind of ping pong the three of us played that day. After the games, as was our practice in good weather, we joined Stephen and Barb on their outside patio, ordered Chinese take-out, joked around, as we were wont to do, things on the surface the same as always, except for this one thing. Stephen had decided to die, to fast himself to death. Uncharted waters, indeed. "It's the end of an era," C.J. had said, back in the garage.

Yet here was this beautiful spring evening, Stephen looking happy, talking about everyday things. Then, off-hand like, he surprised me by asking what I thought of his decision to die. "I don't like it," I was shocked to hear myself say, since it was the exact opposite of what I'd been thinking, full of admiration for his taking the bull by the horns, for choosing his moment.

A couple of days later Stephen had a last meal with Barbara. C.J. cooked it and brought it over. There was not even a hint of melodrama around the event, Barbara said. It was the same, as I heard said, for those of us who spent a final hour with him at his bedside. In Stephen's and my good-bye visit, he spoke words of praise for our longstanding ping pong group, how well we all had gotten on together. We talked about the NBA playoffs. They were helping him pass the time, he said. When it was time to go, we shook hands firmly, held on a little bit, looking into each other's eyes. He said that we'd been good friends. I agreed. "I think it was the sports," he said.

In my first communication with Barbara, several weeks after Stephen died, she wrote that most of the time, for her, Stephen is both simultaneously present and gone, and that she's learning to live in two worlds at once.

And to an obviously lesser degree and in my own way, that has happened to me. Beyond simply remembering him, I have felt his presence a couple of times in an "up there" kind of way. The first was when I arrived one evening to play ping pong. The other players hadn't shown up yet. Behind the garage, the sun was settling into the woods, and a very unusual mood overtook me that had Stephen written all over it.

A couple of weeks after that I was inside the house for the first time since he'd died. Barbara was away. Bryon MacWilliams, a fellow poet, here with us tonight, was dog-sitting. In full view of Stephen's empty chair, we talked long into the evening about who he had been to us. It's not like I actually saw him sitting there, but I must have been staring at that chair in a strange way, or a little too long, when Bryon asked me if I wanted to sit in it.

"The chair? No, no," I said. "I couldn't.... Have you sat in it?"

"Yeah," Bryon said. "It took a couple days, but I sat in it."

But you didn't have to be on his property or in his home to have a Stephen moment. From as far away as San Francisco, Diane Frank, a poet herself and a former student and life-long Stephen Dunn devotee, spoke of palpably feeling his presence. She sent me a poem in which she asked her late father to greet him on the other side. My good friend, Howard Reynolds, on a drive we were taking around Lake Gordon, told me that he'd had a vision of Stephen guiding me as I wrote this eulogy.

How Stephen himself would feel about such perceptions, I have no doubt, for he and I had talked about the afterlife several times. He didn't believe in it for a minute, not in a mysterious form, anyway. One of his favorite quotes was, "Yes, there's another world, and it's in this one."

A few years back, after Kurt Detwiler's Memorial in the Saville Gallery in Cumberland (Kurt was a beloved, longstanding member of our local poetry group), Stephen and I stood next to each other at the hors d'oeuvres table, and without looking up he said "this is the afterlife, Jim. Being remembered."

But whether Stephen was right about that, are we not in these very moments, in this gathering, honoring his afterlife as he envisioned it: being remembered. And in *remembering Stephen together* now, ... well, I'm sure that the thought of us collectively doing just that pleased him, in advance, to no end.

Oh, there'll be poetry readings that include Stephen Dunn for a long time to come. He'll be taught in schools. People who never knew him in person will continue to feel a powerful connection to him through his poetry. I believe that. But will anybody ever remember this Stephen Dunn of a poet as we are remembering him now. By "we" I mean us, this particular collective of souls with whom for nineteen years Stephen lived nearby "in the despoiled and radiant now," in the most ordinary and extraordinary of ways.

About The Author, James (Jim) Ralston

Inspired by Thoreau's *Walden*, especially by the second chapter, "Where I Lived, and What I Lived For," I live in the country on three and a half acres between Rocky Gap and Evitts Creeks, eight miles outside of Cumberland, Maryland.

Across Rocky Gap Creek is the rarely used, but nicely kept up Union Grove Campgrounds, and equally rarely used outdoor pavilion/church, as if they're extensions of both my front yard and spiritual life. Many mornings, I sit in the pavilion alone, meditating, contemplating, writing in my journal. Above the sanctuary, a sign reads, "YE MUST BE BORN AGAIN," and Thoreau and I couldn't agree more. We don't see it as an order from above, rather as something necessary.

Three houses up the creek from my small home is a one-room schoolhouse, like the one in Michigan where my Grandma Nora used to teach. I never walk by it without remembering her and Aunt Emma, who generously shared their small house with me in 1961, so I could afford my first year of Alma College, a Christian college where I lost my little boy faith, I now know, in retrospect, to give myself room for something bigger, thanks Grandma, Aunt Emma, and Alma.

What I have lived *for* is harder to condense, but can be found in my publications, which include *The Choice of Emptiness*, a collection of essays and reflections that also reads as a novel; numerous essays and poems published in *The Sun: a Magazine of Ideas* over a span 35 years; and fifteen years of columns published between 1990 and 2005 in the Charleston *Gazette*, and in this book of poems, and an earlier one, *Lyrics for a Low Noon*, both published by Blue Light Press out of San Francisco.

Along the way, I also directed many plays in several theatres, but primarily in the Apollo Theater in Martinsburg, West Virginia. Several of the plays I wrote myself, including "Many Mansions," "The Lone Star League," and "Divine Madness."

www.ingramcontent.com/pod-product-compliance
Lightning Source LLC
Chambersburg PA
CBHW032007080426
42735CB00007B/540